Random Features

Each face offers up clues to the mysteries of the human heart; but they are only clues. A face reveals much more than the uniqueness of its features—and one cannot look close enough at each one to know exactly where the person has been, how they think, or what secrets are buried within their soul. We only see expressions they make and then imagine what is really trying to be said. The countenance may emanate from a face, but is it a real articulation—or merely a decoy that lures us from what is carefully being hidden away?

Random Features
Copyright © 2016 Charles A. Dean

Printed in the United States of America

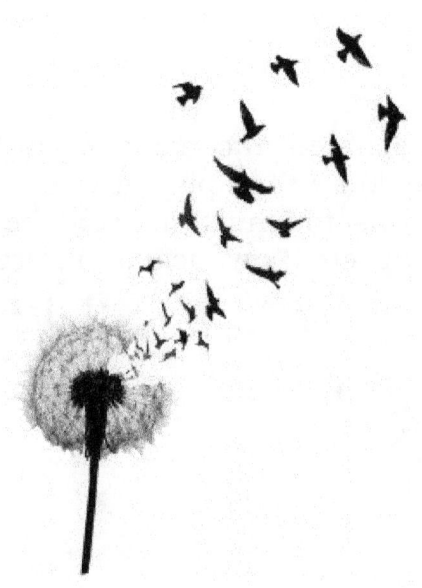

They hesitated to consider what had drawn them close. More than play; it was a deep sense of two worlds touching. It went beyond what they had expected; mystical and pure.

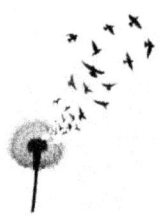

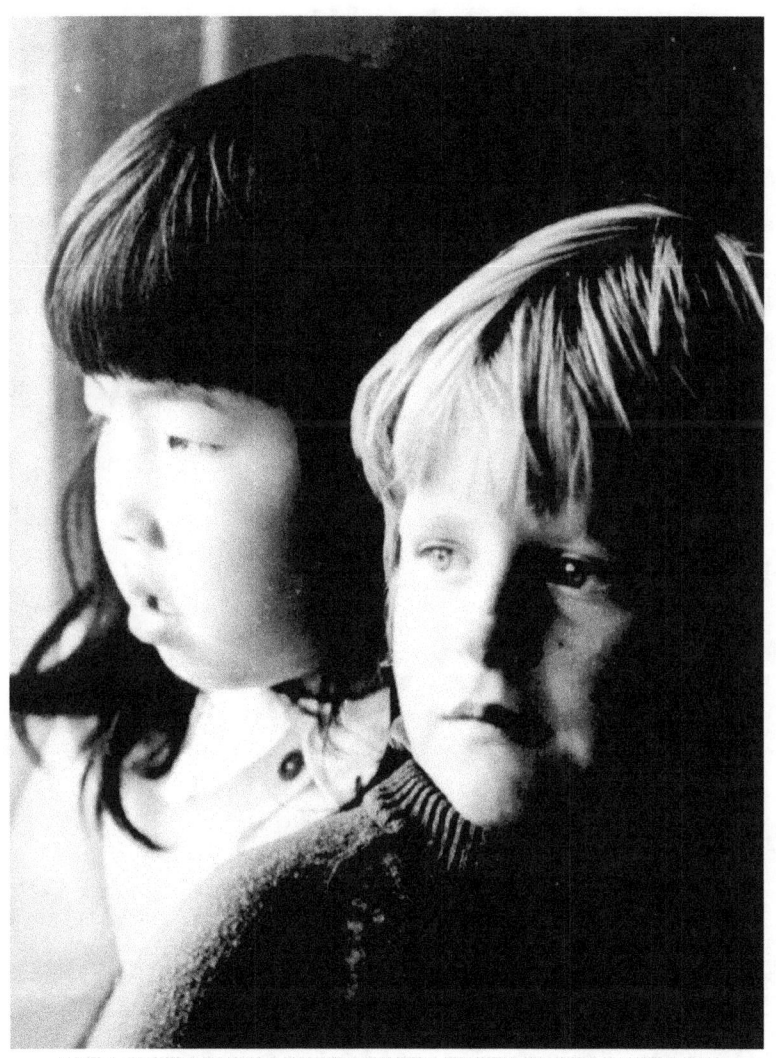

An honest heart compelling a life—few inhabit such a world.

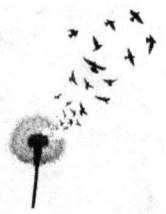

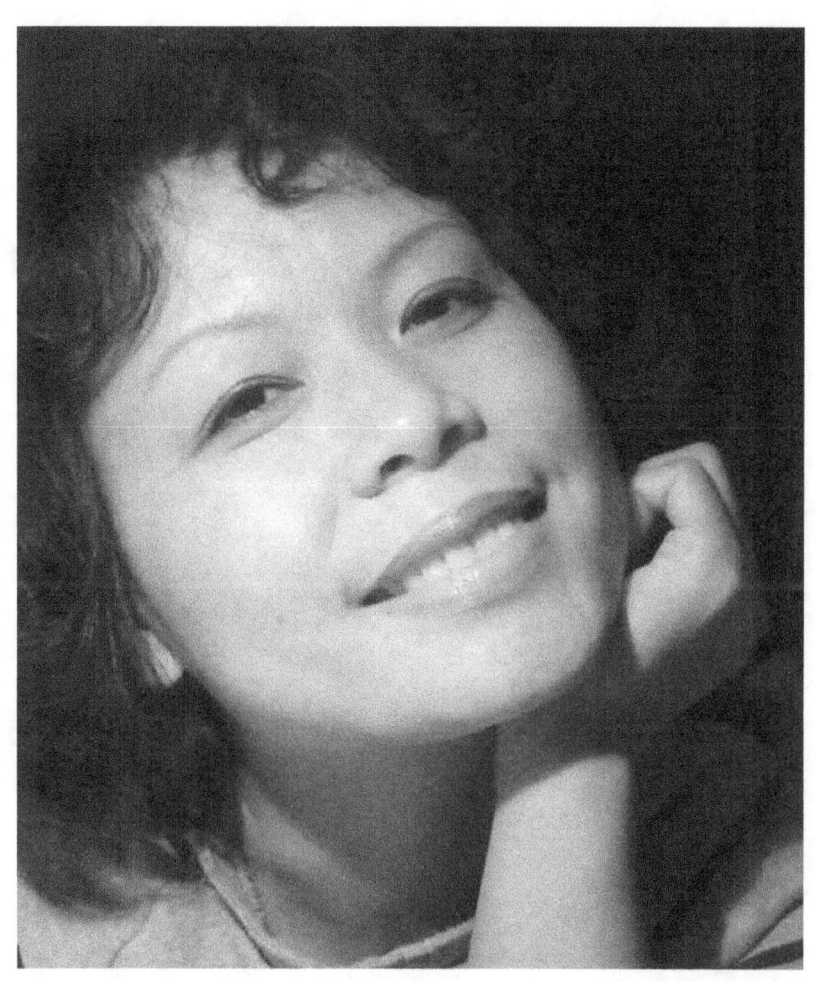

Perhaps it was curiosity that brought you; or perhaps it was a stellar compass that directed you to my door.

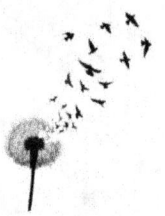

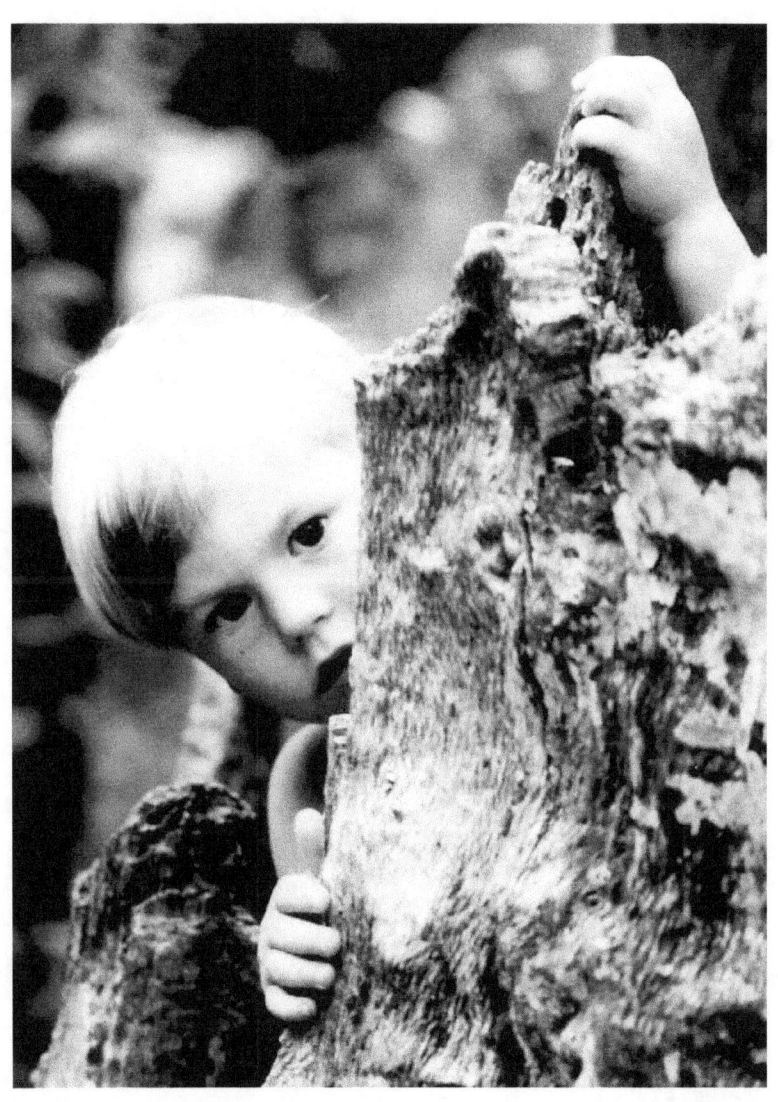

I saw you; we never spoke. There were many things we each wanted to know but the words had escaped us.

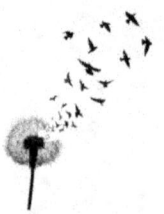

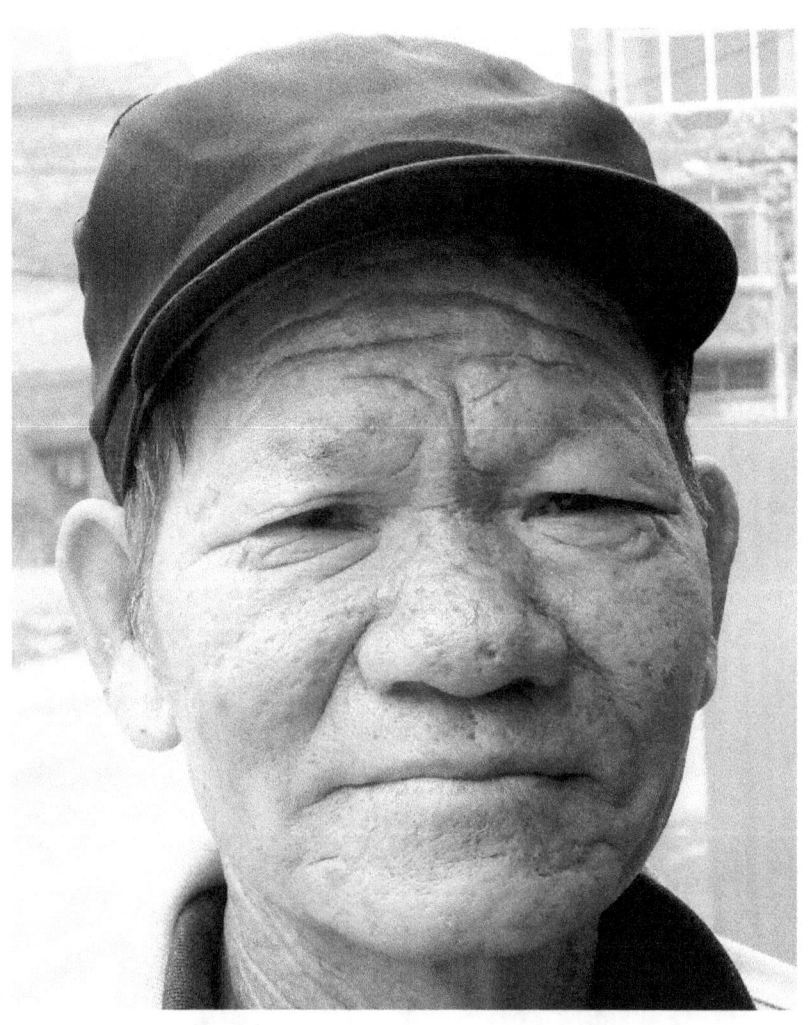

Wondering can be done while life goes on.

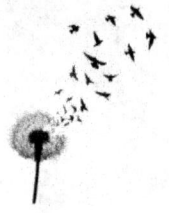

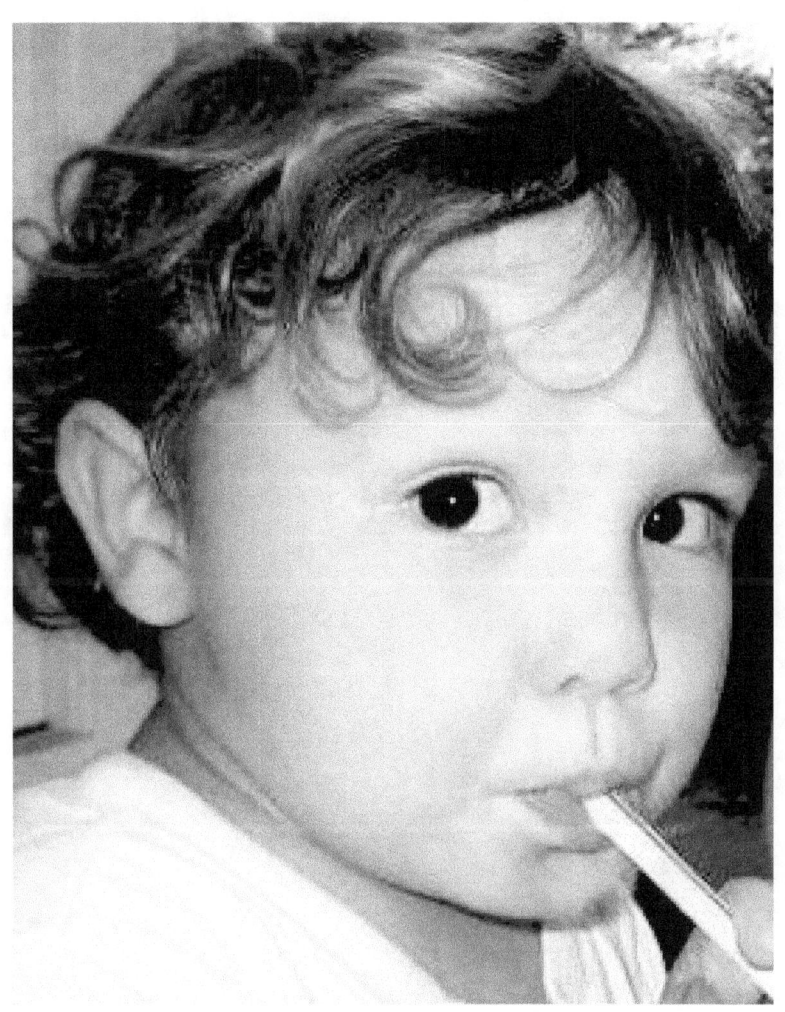

She suddenly emerged as a woman, but somehow we missed the moment that it happened. It was clear she had become passionate and mortal, and her voice rang out, "Yeah, yeah..."

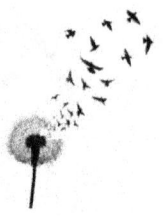

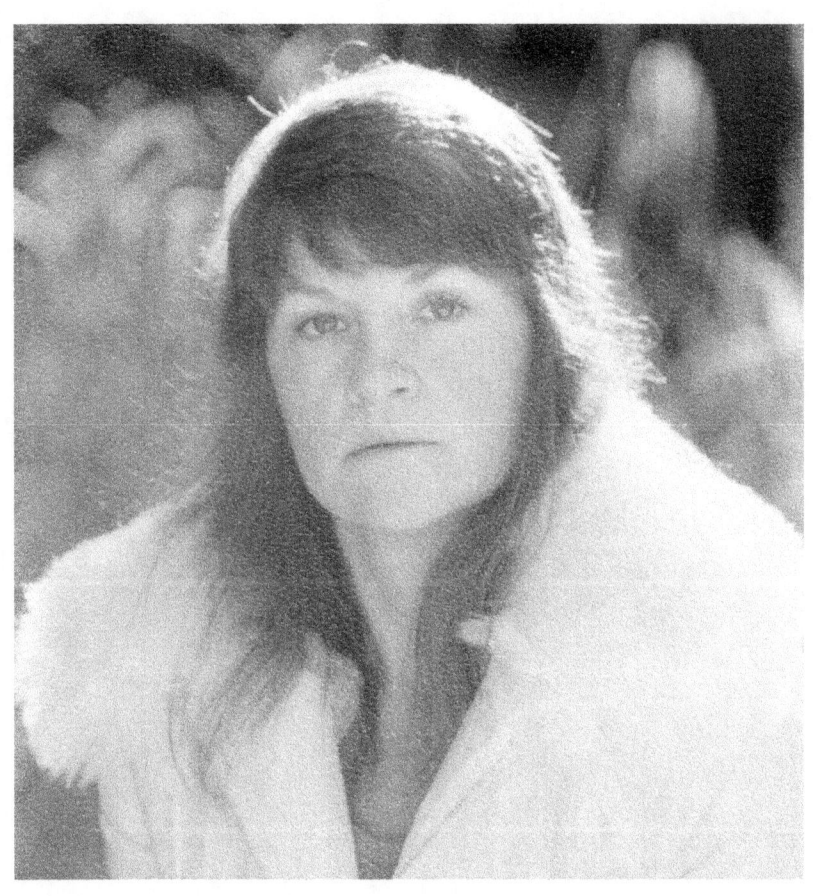

Old city...older than my home, and you beckoned me. Each step taken in your presence is cushioned with wonder. Such beauty frayed by time.

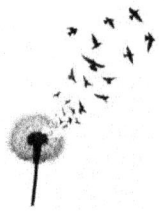

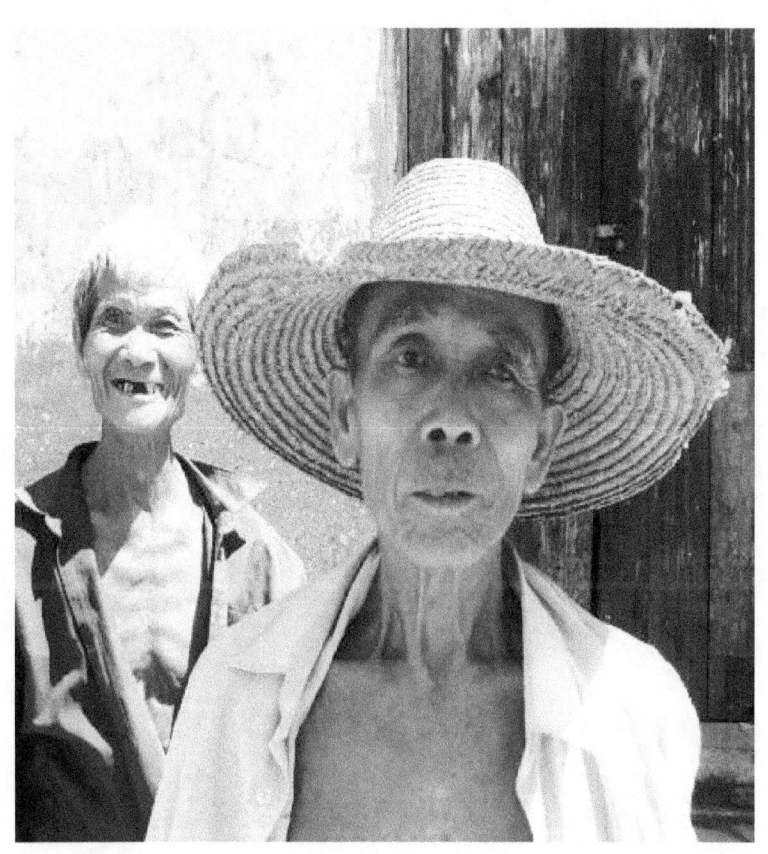

The seeker, my friend...made from two bands half a world apart. The last of the bears with skillful paws to make wondrous things.

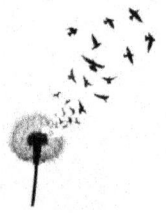

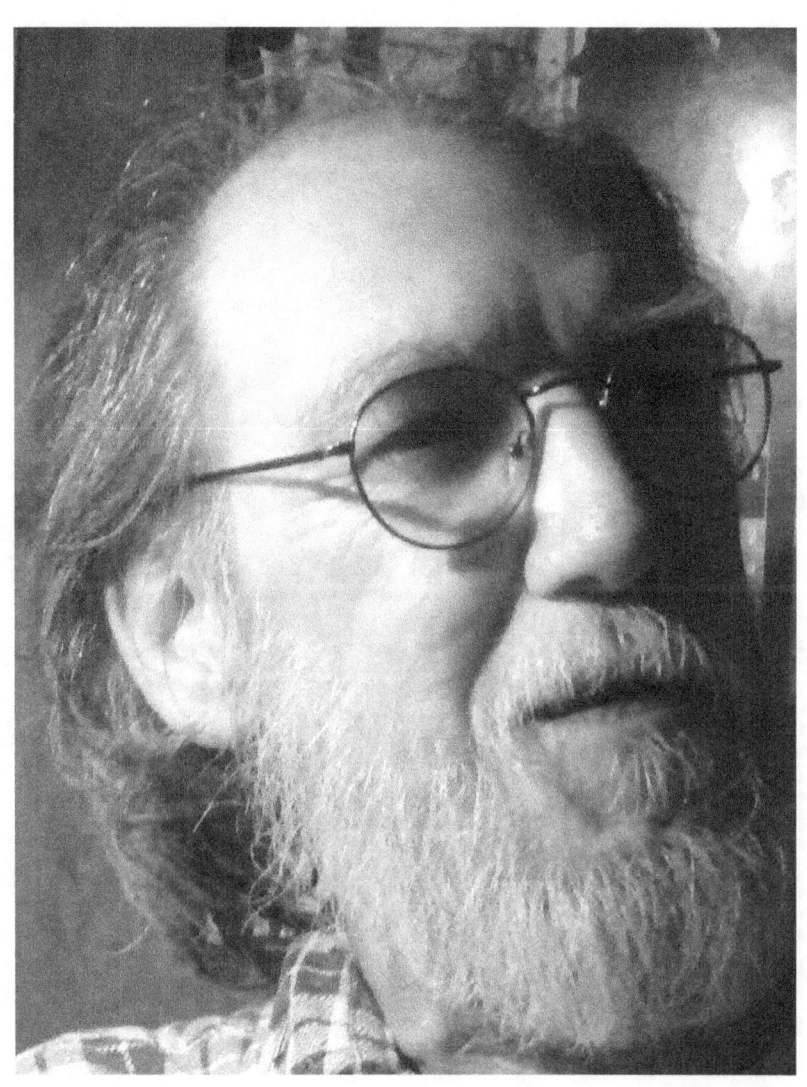

Happiness etched in rough hews, beautiful throughout time. You offered me more than I deserved, and I was changed forever.

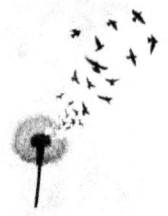

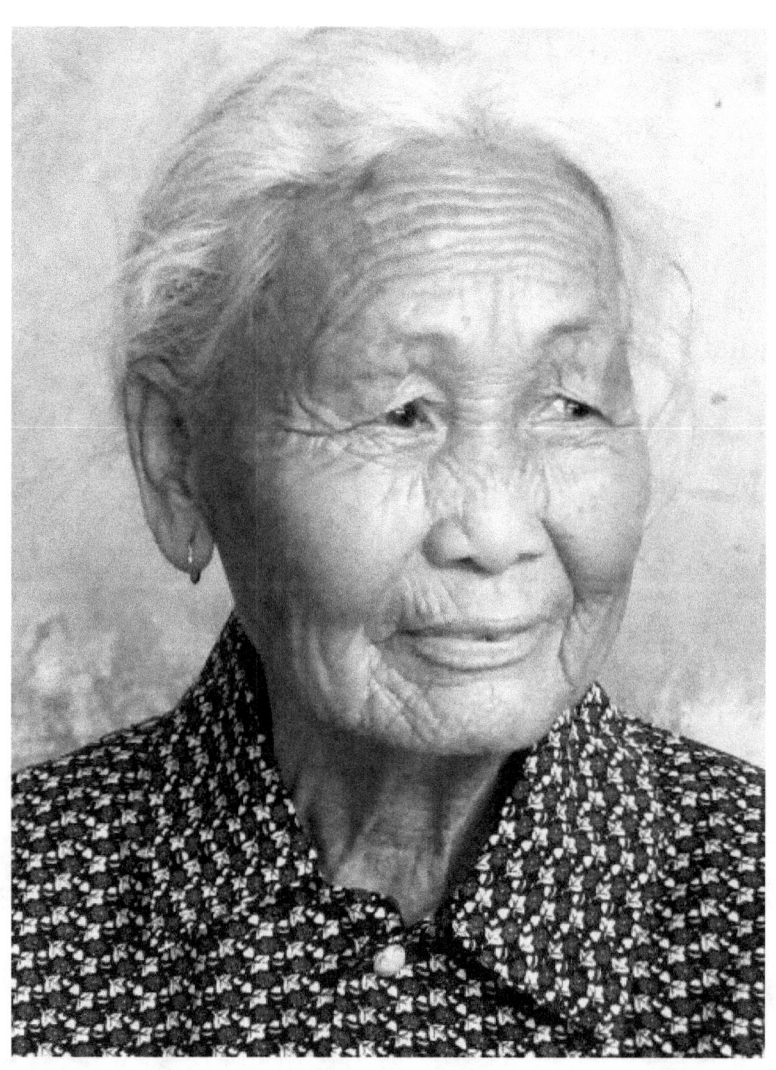

Like soft fluffy clouds drifting slowly through the skies, you watch the horizon quietly for what is to come.

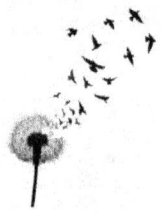

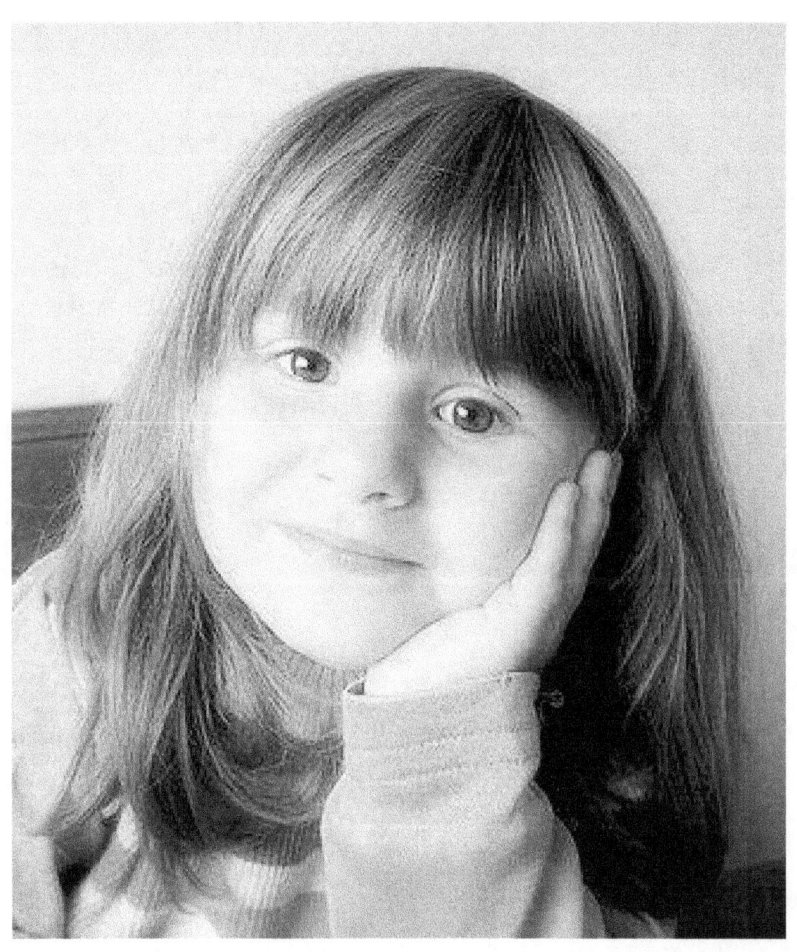

Walking with ease facing the wind; this bravery is not in fighting, but from the strength that is within.

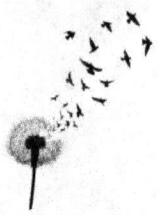

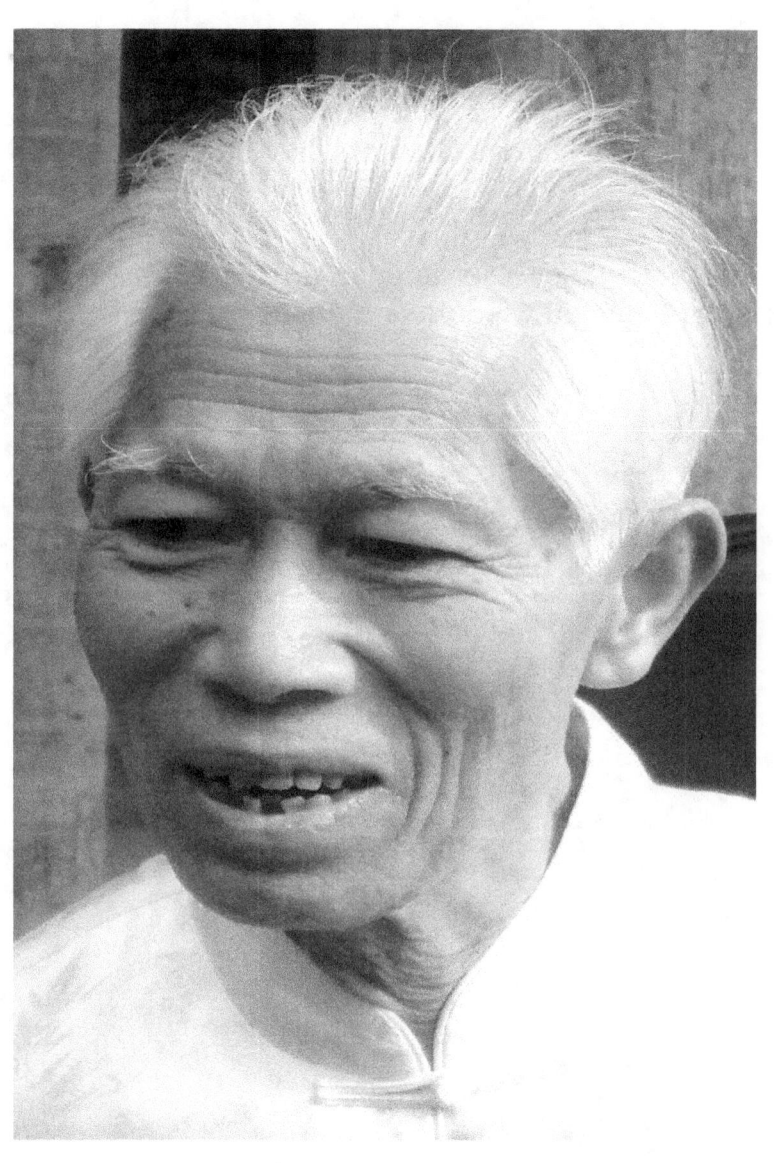

Quietly does the listener do his trade. The mark of eternal wisdom is a silent presence.

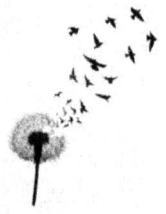

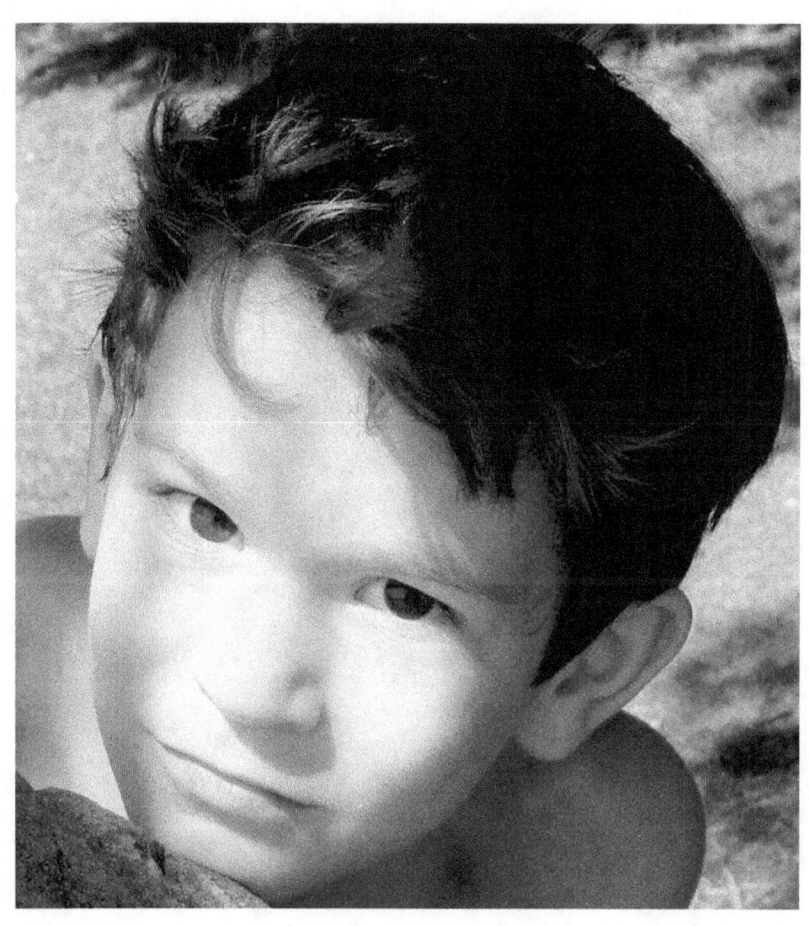

As weapons are stacked and battles wind down, may your hands reclaim their gentle expression of love.

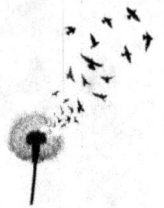

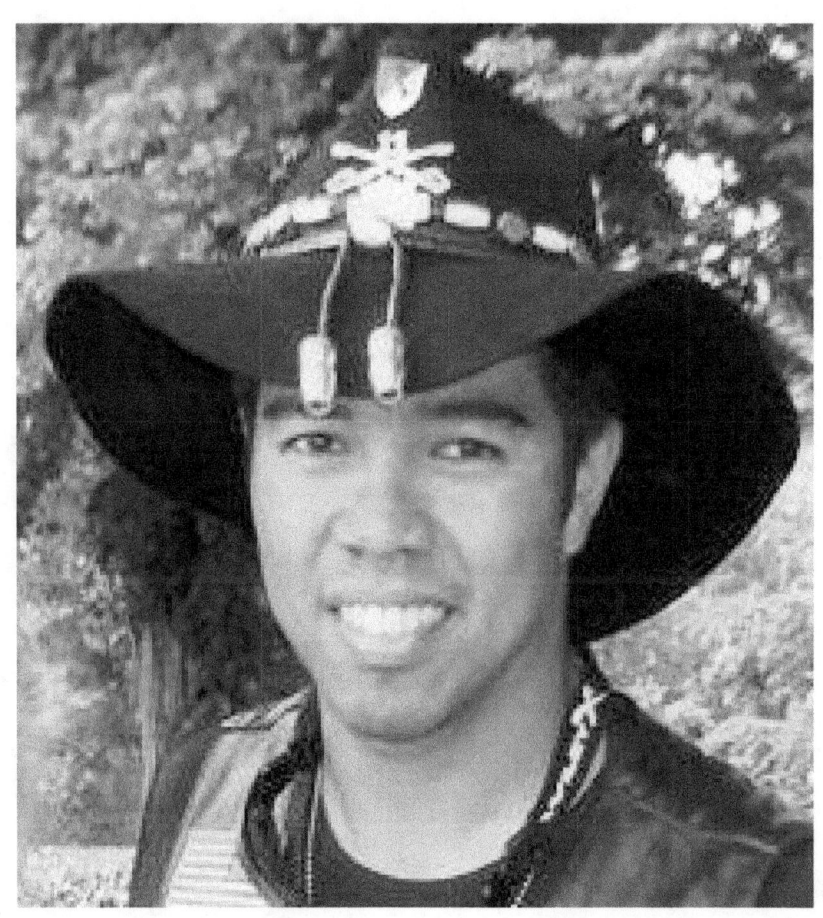

The light tapping on my door brings tears of joy...you have always known how to make me love again and again. As we danced I learned to cry, but you never understood why.

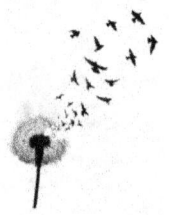

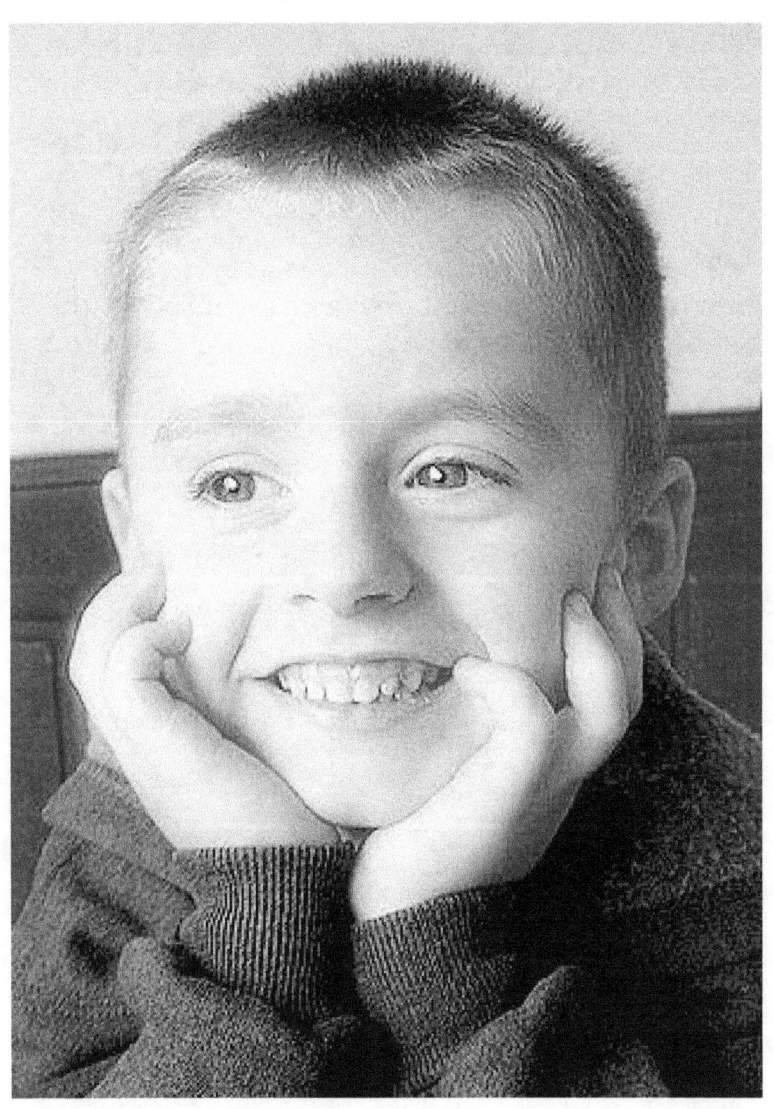

The absent footprints doesn't mean I've never been there. A happy heart shared is the best of all marks to leave.

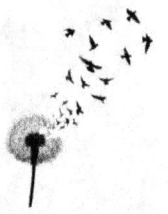

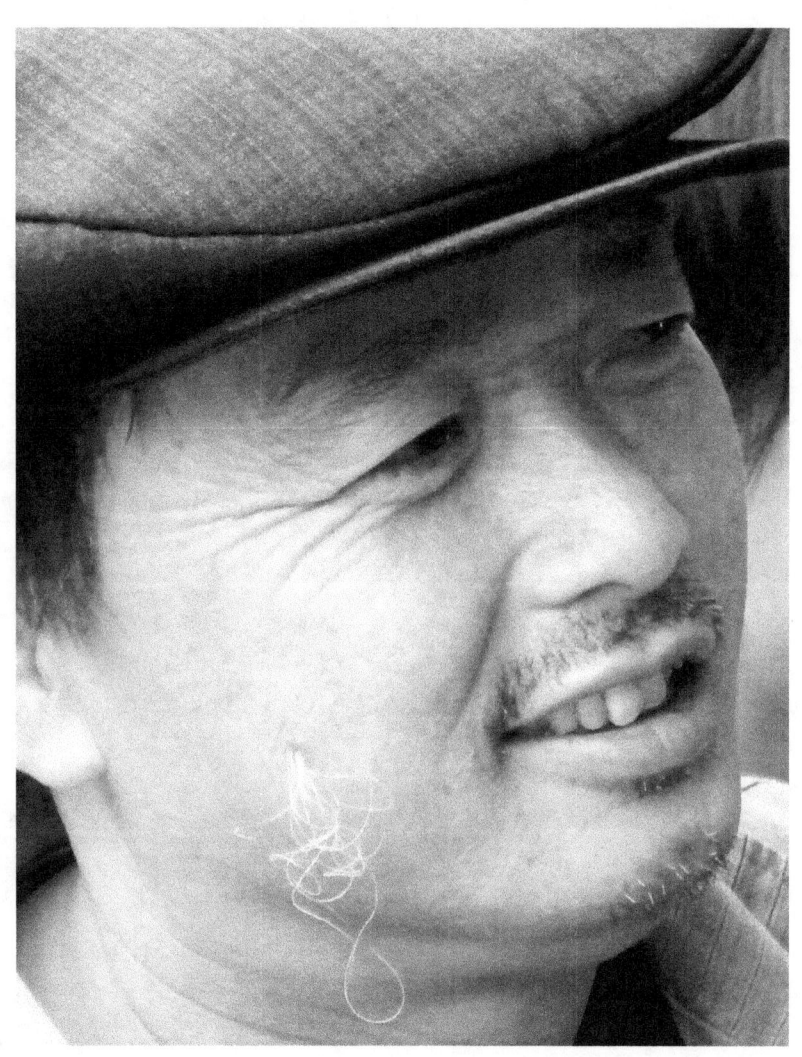

A brilliant world built from simple, certain things; like certain faces glowing with certain royalty that commands a certain audience—certainly to behold.

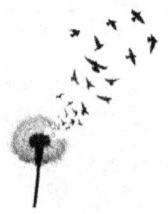

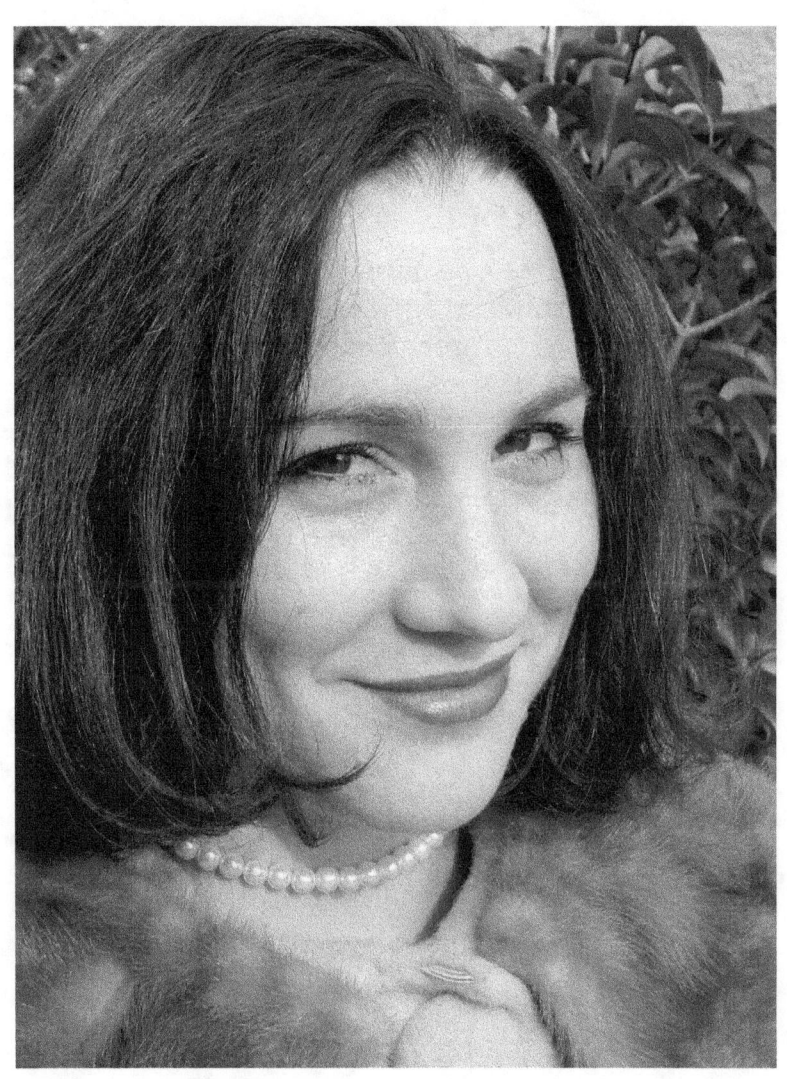

The silence of the sun seems to overcome the noise of the sea...the rushing current is stilled by your inner peace. Watering and turning the soil of those in his charge, he longs for the one line they will remember always...one that is more precious than anything they might own. It is yet to come...

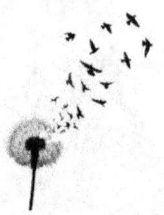

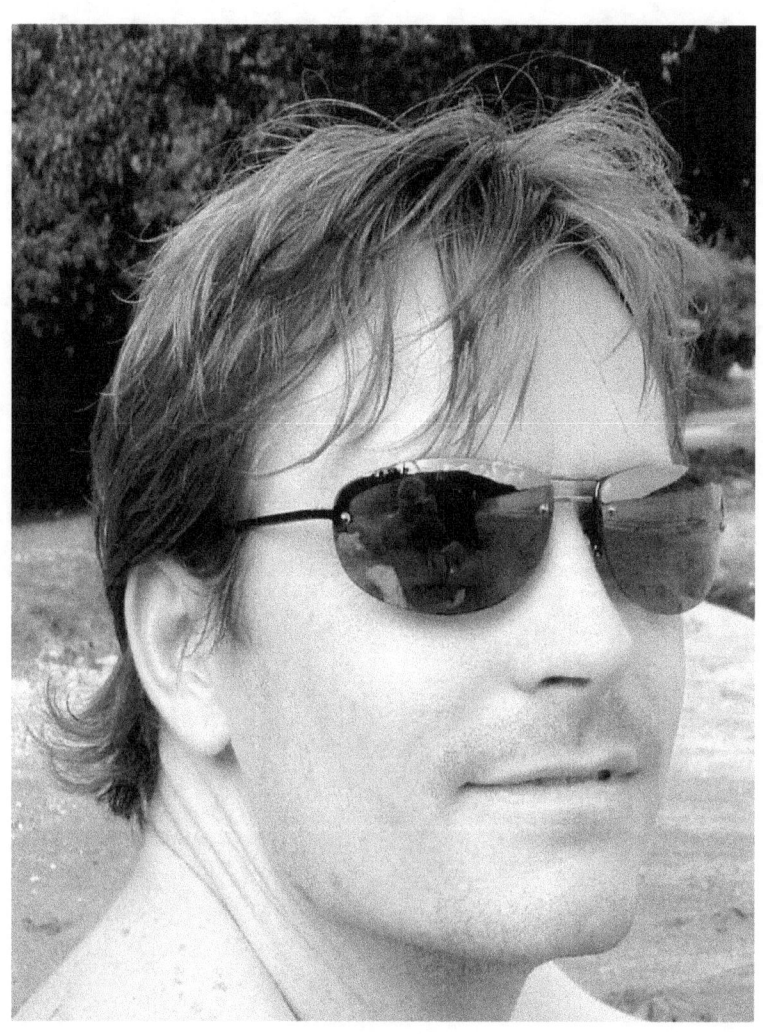

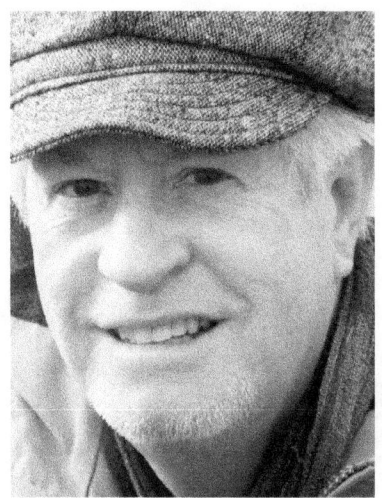

Chuck Dean

Chuck Dean is the author of numerous books, including *Nam Vet: Making Peace with Your Past, Down Range to Iraq and Back, Some Came Home,* and *Inside Shadows.* In 2008 he was awarded the Leadership Award by the Hirsch Foundation for his writing and work in the veteran community. At one point in his career he worked as a free-lance photographer, and this book is dedicated to those times.

All of his books are available at:
www.amazon.com/author/chuckdeanbooks